CW00474190

New Zealand Travel Guide

The Top 10 Highlights in New Zealand

Table of Contents

Introduction to New Zealand

New Zealand is a photogenic, otherworldly country that offers visitors incomparable options for exploration and adventure. A place where traditional Maori culture mixes with the modernity of cosmopolitan cities, pleasant villages and the vast expanse of unspoiled wilderness, New Zealand offers plenty of attractions to suit any traveler.

Fiordland National Park is home to Milford Sound, which offers some of the most staggering coastal scenery in the world, with its dark blue waters and dramatic peaks. The frequent downpours of the region only enhance the beauty of Milford Sound, as they send many waterfalls cascading down its cliffs.

The Bay of Islands is a picturesque region that is home to 144 islands, numerous secluded bays and some amazing sandy beaches. The beautiful bay boasts an abundance of marine life including penguins, dolphins, whales and big marlin. The breathtaking scenery of the Bay of Islands can only be appreciated by taking a cruise through the area.

The Abel Tasman National Park is a hiker's dream, with one of the sunniest climates and top coastal scenery in the country. Closed to vehicles, you will have to enter on foot, by boat or small plane, but the trip will be well worth it. As you traverse the mountainous terrain, you will be treated to sightings of blue penguins, oyster catchers, wood pigeons and other rare birds.

Kaikoura is a small coastal town that's a haven for lovers of seafood. Here you can spot sperm whales, fur seals, albatrosses and dolphins off the shore, and later indulge in a feast of fresh blue cod, crayfish or mussels. Nature lovers can take a wilderness stroll through the dramatic and untamed Kaikoura forest.

The Westland National Park is home to the Franz Josef Glacier, one of the most accessible of its kind in the world. Visitors are able to walk right up to the foot of this massive glacier, or even take a helicopter ride over the dazzling Ice Age relic. Along with the Fox Glacier, Franz Josef is one of the major tourist draws in the region.

Rotorua is regarded as New Zealand's thermal wonderland due to its many hot springs and geysers situated in and around the city, mainly within the nature reserves and parks. Natural eruptions of hot water, steam and mud occasionally occur in new locations here. Close by is another popular attraction, the Waiotapu, with its numerous hot springs famous for their colorful appearance.

Tongariro National Park is famous for its extremes and surprises. The park features a diverse range of ecosystems that include desert-like plateaus, active volcanoes, untamed forests, tranquil lakes and herb fields. Go hiking to the stunning Taranaki Falls, through forest and scrubland and across a lava line of volcanic eruptions dating from hundreds of years ago.

New Zealand draws many with its pristine atmosphere, fantastic scenery and extraordinary landscapes. From the rugged islands with dense native forests, to the thermal regions, mountains, glaciers, beaches and well-preserved fjords, it's impossible to run out of things to see and do in New Zealand. Heavenly and pristine, the island nation of New Zealand has something for everyone - including you.

1. Bay of Islands

The Bay of Islands in New Zealand offers a combination of unique, stunning scenery and important history. With 144 islands enclosed within it, the Bay of Islands is a paradise for water sports lovers with its opportunities for sailing, diving and more. And being close to the top of New Zealand, its mild, subtropical climate makes it ideal to visit any time in the year.

Situated about three and a half hours drive from Auckland, the Bay of Islands is found in the Northland region of New Zealand, on the eastern coast of the North Island. This is the side with the sheltered coastline and all the pretty bays in which most water activities in New Zealand are enjoyed. The Bay of Islands is also home to several small settlements, each with its own attractions and character.

There's plenty to see and do in the Bay of Islands. Everywhere on land, there are great walks to take and trails to explore. There are also numerous vantage points that offer magnificent views of the Bay. Inland from Kerikeri is the Puketi Forest, one of the largest areas of ancient kauri forest within the Northland.

Take boat trip or go on an island cruise which includes visiting the famous "Hole in the Rock". Have some lunch and relax as you leisurely enjoy the water. Visit some of the islands and cruise through the "Hole in the Rock". You can also enjoy sailing trips, snorkeling and diving. Russell, Paihia and many of the other Bay Islands feature nice beaches for sunbathing and swimming.

Also take an archaeological walk at Urapukapuka Island on which you can discover ancient Maori sites and the unique natural features of the Bay's largest island.

There is also a lot of history to the Bay Islands. Russell, Waitangi and Kerikeri are among the most historic settlements in New Zealand. The islands are home to numerous buildings and places of interest that trace the development of Maori and European settlement in the country. You will also find plenty of restaurants and cafés in Kerikeri, Russell and Paihia.

You could also take the Ninety Mile Beach Coach Trip that will take you from Paihia to Cape Reinga at New Zealand's northern tip and back again. During the journey, you will visit beaches while driving along the Ninety Mile Beach, which is the only beach in the country that is part of the national highway network. If you don't have time to explore the Far North on your own, this is a great option with informative commentary along the way.

To enjoy New Zealand art and shop for souvenirs, visit Cabbage Tree on Paihia. Roughly twenty minutes drive south of Paihia are the Kawiti Glow Worm Caves. The caves are full of glow worms and interesting limestone formations.

You can also take the Paihia to Opua Coastal Walk that follows the coast from Paihia south to the Opua port. It offers a combination of beach walking, some coastal climbs for stunning views, and a boardwalk through mangroves.

Mount Bledisloe is a unique viewing spot situated behind Waitangi, a short walk from the road. Here you can enjoy almost 360-degree views that take in the Waitangi forest behind as well as the entire Bay.

Pompallier House in Russell is a museum that was once home to the first catholic mission in New Zealand. Built in 1842, the house features a printing press that is worth a look.

Kemp House in Kerikeri is the oldest surviving wooden building in New Zealand, a remnant of the nation's first European settlement. Next door to it is the Stone Store, another old building constructed in 1832.

The Church and Mission House at Waimate North are situated inland from Kerikeri within a delightful rural setting and are all that remain of one of the country's earliest European settlements. Mission House is the second-oldest wooden building in New Zealand, while the adjacent church was built in 1871.

2. Fiordland National Park

Fiordland is one of the most remote and special regions of New Zealand. Home to world famous attractions such as Milford Sound, Lake Te Anau and Doubtful Sound, the national park of Fiordland boasts some of the country's most spectacular scenery.

Situated in the southwestern corner of the South Island, Fiordland is largely comprised of the Fiordland National Park. The Park encloses virtually all of the regions Mountains including the southern end of the Southern Alps, lakes, fjords and forests.

The Fiordland National Park is the largest of New Zealand's 14 national parks and was founded in 1952. The Park takes up a major section of Te Wahipounamu and is home to the country's tallest waterfall, the Browne Falls, as well as the 3 deepest lakes: Lake Te Anau, Lake Hauroko and Lake Manapouri. The Park also boasts some of the most pristine landscapes of New Zealand.

Fiordland owes its name to its fjords characterized by deep river valleys that run to the sea, and which were carved out by glaciers millions of years ago. These fjords are called "sounds" - the most famous of which are Milford Sound and Doubtful Sound.

One of the most amazing travel destinations in the world, Milford Sound and its majestic Mitre Peak are an international landmark. Some of the popular activities to do here include walking, hiking, kayaking and taking boat cruises. Doubtful Sound is the second largest fjord in Fiordland and also a marine reserve. Visitors can take a boat cruise on the Sound, departing from Te Anau across Lake Manapouri.

Lake Te Anau is the second deepest and second largest lake in New Zealand, which is a popular base for hiking and sightseeing. The town also has restaurants and other good amenities.

The Fiordland National Park boasts numerous amazing opportunities for taking walks or going on hikes. The Park features 3 of New Zealand's Nine Great Walks: the 4-day Milford Track; the 3-4 day Kepler Track and the 2-3 day Routeburn Track. The 3-day Hollyford Track is another pleasant walking trail among many others of varying lengths found here.

While most visitors come during summer, Fiordland is also worth visiting during other times of the year. During spring, the flowering alpine plants make for a spectacular sight. One of the wettest places in the world, Fiordland experiences very high rainfall.

3. Waitomo Glow Worm Caves

Situated about three and a half hours drive from Auckland, the Waitomo Glow Worm Caves are a must for visitors to New Zealand. The journey from Auckland to the Waitomo Caves makes for a scenic drive past a lovely countryside with green, rolling hills and numerous flowering trees. If visiting during spring, you will encounter gorgeous farmland where everything is green and high mountains in the distance.

Visitors can tour the Waitomo Glow Worm Caves by walking or taking a boat ride. Another good way to tour the caves is via the 3-hour black water rafting tour which will take you through narrow passages with low ceilings. This tubing tour is ideal for energetic adventure seekers.

A guide will lead you during your walking tour down steps inside a softly lit cave that offers a lovely ambience. Your guide may stress on your need to be silent as the glow worms tend to turn off their bioluminescence when they are stressed.

Under a huge rock hanging just about 2 feet from the floor you will see thousands of little mono-filament-like lines, each about a foot or so long. The lines are suspended from the rock and glisten in the soft light. The lines are in fact the glow worms who are fishing with their lines.

The glow worms are actually larvae that attach themselves to rock and build thin lines with slimy, sticky secretions. Just as in a spider web, small bugs get caught in the line and the glow worm reels them in and eats them.

Your tour will end with a short boat ride out of the caves. You will float silently through a huge cavern inside the caves, your guide using a suspended rope to pull you quietly along the route.

Soon you will leave the soft lights and find yourself in complete darkness. Look up and high overhead you will see millions of glowing dots of light. Because it is completely dark, you won't be able to see the fishing lines, just the glowing larvae of the glow worms. The sight is quite magical, almost like you are looking through a very dense, large tree on a full moon night.

4. Westland Tai Poutini National Park

The Westland Tai Poutini National Park enables visitors to release their inner explorer in a pristine environment that offers a wide selection of impressive and tempting terrain. Here you will find peaks towering at 3,000m over lowland rainforests that reach all the way to the edges of the Tasman Sea. The area is also blessed with contrasting tussock grasslands, lakes, coast, rivers and wetlands.

Also known as glacier country, the Westland Tai Poutini National Park has in some places, huge tongues of ice extending all the way back down close to sea level. The biggest draws to the Westland Tai Poutini National Park are the Franz Josef and Fox glaciers.

For the majority of travelers, the fast-moving Franz Josef and Fox glaciers are the primary reason for visiting. They move up to 4 meters each day, which in the world of glaciers is uncommonly rapid. At the foot of each glacier, you can hear the crushing, grinding sounds of ancient ice forcing itself down the time-worn valleys.

There are various ways of experiencing the glaciers. You may walk to the terminus of either glacier, or hike through the bush to a viewing point. Another option is to join a guided glacier walk for which ice climbing equipment will be provided. The third option is to take to the air and view the glaciers from a helicopter or small plane.

While glaciers around the world are retreating, the Franz Josef and Fox glaciers continue flowing almost to sea level. The temperate climate at this low altitude makes these glaciers among the most convenient to visit in the world.

Between the sea and the glaciers, the park is also a bird watcher's paradise. The rainforests and vast areas of wetland shelter rare species of birds. Take an easy stroll to the base of the fascinating Franz Josef and Fox glaciers and spot some of the rarest native birds of New Zealand in the wetlands and rainforests.

During the nesting season, a local guide can take you to see the beautiful white herons in the Waitangi Roto Nature Reserve. You can also go kayaking on the lakes or in the Okarito lagoon where you can also spy the bird life.

Visitors to the Westland Tai Poutini National Park can also embark on kayaking adventures on Lake Matheson and Mapourika, as well as explore coastal lagoons and vast rivers. You can also go on one day treks to the Welcome Flat hot pools. Mountaineers may enjoy the historic Copland Track which crosses the great divide.

The Southern Alps Mountains are revered by the local Maori people, the Ngai Tahu, as their ancestors. The entire coastal environment is also of considerable importance to the people, both spiritually, and for the food and resources it provides.

5. Rotorua

Rotorua is a region of great diversity in activities, attractions and cultures. Begin your tour of Rotorua attractions at Waimangu Thermal Valley, an active volcanic area southeast of the city. The Boiling Lake at Waimangu Thermal Valley is one of the world's largest boiling lakes set in the heart of the geothermal region.

Rotorua boasts geysers, mud pools, boiling water streams and multi-colored landscapes of the city's geothermal spots. Of the various areas devoted to geothermal observation, the closest is in Whakarewarewa.

The Bubbling Geothermal Mud Whakarewarewa is characterized by hot mud pools that are a sight to behold. The pools resemble huge ridged pancakes on a moonscape and give loud plopping sounds as their bubbles surface. Also in the reserve are unique geothermal vegetation, geysers, silica terraces, bush walks, a kiwi house and cultural center.

Also at Whakarewarewa is Phohutu, a spectacular geyser that erupts throughout the day, bubbling up from below ground and shooting up to 30 meters high, while displaying the amazing powers of nature.

Visitors to Rotorua can also go cycling in New Zealand's forests. Be it wide open spaces or lush forest tracks, cycling is a great way of getting close to nature and exploring the richly varied countryside of New Zealand. You can explore the Redwood forest in Whakarewarewa, which offers over 30 km of cycle trails, just a 10 minute ride from the Rotorua city center.

Adventure lovers can go whitewater rafting on the Kaituna River, home to the highest commercially rafted waterfall in the world. Or go zorbing down a steep hillside inside a large air filled rubber ball. Zorbing is another kiwi adventure experience that is becoming one of Rotorua's most popular activities.

There are also plenty of opportunities for outdoor sports including whitewater rafting, mountain biking, parasailing, skydiving, and many more.

Enjoy a spa treatment using the famous Rotorua mud or soak up inside a mineral hot pool. Since ancient times, the indigenous peoples have used the waters for their therapeutic qualities.

Rotorua is one of the best places in New Zealand to learn about the Maori people, their history and culture. While here, you can attend a Maori cultural performance or visit a Maori village. Be sure to try a hangi, which is the traditional Maori meal.

Your visit to Rotorua will not be complete without a look at Maori arts and crafts. Visit the New Zealand Maori Arts and Crafts Institute for a glimpse at objects that reflect traditional Maori culture. You can also watch the craftspeople at work and shop for some high-quality souvenirs.

Maori culture is rich in tradition and dancing is an intrinsic part of Maori culture. Visit a traditional hangi where you can watch a performance of Maori folk dancing. The traditional poi dance is one of the most popular cultural dances.

Rotorua offers a wide range of things to see and do, both indoors and outdoors. There are also a wide range of places to eat in Rotorua.

Even more spectacular natural wonders await you outside of Rotorua. Situated about 27 kilometers south of Rotorua is the Waiotapu active geothermal area. The area features numerous hot springs famous for their colorful appearance arising from the dramatic geothermal conditions. In addition to the colorful hot springs, there are geysers, pools and boiling mud pools. Be sure to check out Lady Knox Geyser, Champagne Pool, Primrose Terrace and Artist's Palette.

6. Tongariro National Park

Situated in the center of North Island, the Tongariro National Park is one of the most important natural areas in New Zealand, and one of international repute. The country's oldest national park, Tongariro was also the fourth national park to be established anywhere in the world.

The site is recognized for both its natural and cultural significance, and features the Tongariro Crossing, New Zealand's most popular walk. The Park is located just a short distance to the south west from Lake Taupo, which many visitors use as a base for exploring the area.

The region of Tongariro National Park, in particular the 3 mountains, are of great significance to the local Maori ethnic group, the Ngati Tuwharetoa. The oldest building inside the park is the Chateau Tongariro, a large hotel that was built in 1929.

The Park's most dramatic features are 3 active volcanoes: Tongariro, Ngauruhoe and Ruapehu, which are the focal point of the entire central North Island. Tongariro River is the main river that feeds Lake Taupo and which has its beginnings in the mountains. There is an abundance of tracks and streams to explore in this area.

One of the most distinctive aspects of the Tongariro National Park landscape is the tussock grass that covers large areas of open ground. These are low native grasses that do well in elevated pine areas of the park that surround the mountains. The park also has forest areas with large numbers of kanuka and native beech trees. Only lichens are able to survive at the highest areas of the park.

The Park's Birdlife is also very distinctive. Due to its remote location, the Park boasts a wide variety of native birds, including the bellbird, tui and a number of rare species of kiwi. There is also red deer in the Park.

A very special part of New Zealand, the Tongariro National Park is well worth a visit at any time of the year. There's a lot to do in Tongariro National Park, both during summer and winter months.

The main activities during winter are skiing and snowboarding at Whakapapa or Turoa, the two ski fields of the Park situated on the Mount Ruapehu slopes. During the summer, visitors can go mountain biking, hiking or exploring the numerous trails found throughout the park.

7. Auckland

Auckland is the largest city in New Zealand and the place at which most air travelers first arrive. Home to about 1.5 million residents, a third of the population of New Zealand, Auckland has everything you'd expect from a world-class city: a diverse array of bars, cafés, restaurants, culture and entertainment. Also, due to its location, Auckland has a wide choice of outdoor activities to offer.

Rated severally amongst "the top 10 cities in the world to live in", Auckland was well populated with indigenous Maori people before the arrival of the Europeans, due to its fertile soils and proximity to the sea. Auckland became the capital city of New Zealand in 1842, but lost this title in 1876 to the current capital, Wellington.

A vibrant international city, Auckland and its wider surrounding region offers plenty to see and do.

Visitors to Auckland cannot leave without climbing the Sky Tower. Standing at a height of 327 meters, the Sky Tower is the tallest building in the Southern Hemisphere which offers stunning views of the city and its surroundings. The building features 3 levels of observation decks, as well as 3 restaurants with cuisines that range from casual to fine dining.

Adventure lovers will find excitement on an outside walk around the perimeter or a bungee jump, both of which can be experienced from 192 meters above ground. Nonetheless, simply standing on the clear glass plates set into the floor of the observation lounge will give you as much thrills, as your view goes straight down to the street below.

The Auckland harbor is peppered with many islands that are easy to reach via a short ferry ride. On Waiheke Island, visitors can enjoy some wine tasting and beach hopping. On Kawau you can visit the original residence of the Auckland governor, while the Rangitoto summit can be hiked for great views of the city.

The Viaduct harbor area is full of great restaurants in a fantastic setting, right on the waterfront of central Auckland with its distinct nautical atmosphere.

From the city center, a string of 4 lovely beaches ends at St. Heliers Village. Its unique village atmosphere makes for a great spot to end a cycle along the Auckland waterfront.

Ponsonby Road is the trendiest suburb in Auckland whose main street has numerous cafés and bars. There are also plenty of shopping opportunities here.

In contrast to its sheltered eastern coast, Auckland's western coast is rugged and wild. The dramatic black sandy beaches of Karekar, Bethels and Piha are pounded by the rough waters of the Tasman Sea. This makes for a great setting to take long walks and body surf.

Visit the Auckland Museum to learn all about the ancient and recent past of New Zealand through impressive displays of Maori artifacts, natural history and British colonialism, all housed in one of the most impressive buildings in the country. The museum building is set within the Auckland Domain, a large park that is great for having picnics.

The Waitakere Ranges is a unique rainforest to the west of Auckland. The forest features numerous walking trails of varying lengths as well as a scenic railway. The mountainous terrain offers spectacular views of the Tasman Sea to the west and Auckland to the east.

Known as the city of sails, Auckland has a great love affair with yachting. In fact, Auckland has more boats per head of population than anywhere else in the world. On any summer weekend, you will see the Waitemata harbor full of boats on which you can experience sailing.

8. Kaikoura

Kaikoura is situated on the East Coast of New Zealand; about two and a half hours drive from Christ Church. The area itself is steeped in Maori legend and history as it is said that Maui the demi-god fished the North Island from this spot. A small town with a population of about 3,000, Kaikoura draws visitors from around the world with its whale watch cruises.

Whale watching at Kaikoura is one of the main attractions of New Zealand's South Island. Almost half of the 76 species of the world's dolphins and whales have been spotted offshore Kaikoura. The various whales that visit the waters of Kaikoura include the rare migratory humpback whale that is seen mainly in winter and the orca during summer.

The beautiful orcas or "killer whales" are the largest in the dolphin family of animals, growing up to a length of 9.5 meters. While orcas feed on other dolphins, whales and marine creatures, there is no record of an unprovoked attacked on a human by an orca.

Nonetheless, the biggest attraction of the Kaikoura whale watching is the sperm whale. The largest of the toothed whales, sperm whales grow to as much as 20 meters in length.

When the weather and sea conditions allow, the whale watch vessel will push off from Kaikoura. Poor weather prevents the spotter planes from taking off to pinpoint areas of whale activity. Your sailing may therefore be cancelled rather than risk disappointing you in your quest. It is therefore advisable to allow a few days stay in Kaikoura to enable you to take a later cruise in the event of cancellation.

While it is whale watching that has thrust Kaikoura into prominence, the small island town framed by mountains and the Pacific has plenty more attractions and activities to offer. Due to its geological, ecological and geographic features, Kaikoura ranks high in ecotourism. Kaikoura also has restaurants, general stores and souvenir shops that you can visit.

Numerous water activities are also possible in the region including surfing, sailing, swimming, windsurfing, canoeing, whitewater rafting and scuba diving. Land activities include skiing, bushwalks, coastal walks and limestone cave visits.

9. Abel Tasman National Park

The Abel Tasman National Park is the smallest national park in New Zealand which is formed perfectly for adventure and relaxation. The Park is a coastal paradise that enables visitors to walk through or explore via boat or kayak, mixing physical exertion with beach life. Go paddling and hiking, and thereafter sunbathe, swim and indulge in some snorkeling.

Inviting sandy beaches fill the spaces between the tide line and trees. Crystal clear streams tumble down the mossy valleys to join the ocean. Marble and granite formations fringe the headlands which are soaked in native forest.

Te Puketea Bay is a perfect crescent of golden sand with a walking track that leads up Pitt Head to an ancient Maori fort site. Here you can see food pits and terracing that are still visible, and you will understand why the location was chosen as a defensive site once you take in the huge views.

Essential to the scenery is the native wildlife featuring bellbirds and tui whose song fills the forest; cormorants, gannets and little blue penguins diving for dinner; as fur seals lounge on rocks around the edges of the Tonga Island.

The Abel Tasman Coastal Track is classified as one of the "Great Walks" of New Zealand which takes 3-5 days to complete. It climbs around headlands through native forest into a series of beautiful beaches. For a different view of the park, follow the inland tracks leading up to the dramatic karst landscape of the Takaka Hill.

If you crave home comforts, you can stay in the luxurious park lodges, although sleeping under the stars is regarded as the ultimate way of experiencing the spirit of Abel Tasman.

10. Otago

Otago is one of the most diverse and scenic parts of New Zealand, which is home to numerous mountains and lakes. Situated in the far south of South Island, Otago includes much of the southern coastline of South Island. During the summer months, Otago is a Mecca for outdoor activities.

Lakes abound in Otago with some of the most beautiful being Wakatipu, Wanaka, Benmore and Pukaki, along with the Dart, Kawarau and Shotover rivers. The Clutha River flows through Otago and is the largest by volume in New Zealand. All the lakes and rivers offer great recreational opportunities including boating.

Several of the smaller towns like Cromwell, Arrowtown and Dunedin have museums. Visitors can also indulge in skiing and other winter sports.

The vineyards located in Central Otago produce some of the best wines in New Zealand, in particular from the pinot noir grapes. Many wineries are open for tastings with some having restaurants attached. Go on a winery tour which is one of the best ways of discovering Central Otago.

The Otago scenery is awe inspiring and varied, and one of the best things to do in this region is to simply take a car and explore.

You simply cannot take a drive along Otago's northern coastline without taking a stop to marvel at the amazing Moeraki Boulders. Situated at Moeraki are large spherical boulders scattered along the beach, while others emerge from sandstone cliffs. Each of the boulders weighs a few tones and rises up to 2 meters high.

Maori legend has it that the boulders are in fact gourds that were washed ashore from a great voyaging canoe that was wrecked centuries ago. While scientists explain that the boulders are calcite concretions that were formed approximately 65 million years back.

The crystallization of carbonates and calcium around charged particles formed these boulders gradually in a pearl-like process lasting 4 million years. The soft mudstone that contains the boulders was in turn raised about 15 million years ago from the seabed, with the wind, rain and waves excavating the boulders one by one.

There's a viewing platform situated just a couple of minutes walk through a native forest that offers great views of these boulders. If you're lucky you may even see dolphins playing inside the waves near the Moeraki Boulders.

Copyright © 2015. All rights reserved.

Except as permitted under the United States Copyright Act of 1976, reproduction or utilization of this work in any form or by any electronic, mechanical, or other means, now known or hereafter invented, including xerography, photocopying, and recording, and in any information storage and retrieval system, is forbidden without written permission.

The ideas, concepts, and opinions expressed in this book are intended to be used for educational and reference purposes only. Author and publisher claim no responsibility to any person or entity for any liability, loss, or damage caused or alleged to be caused directly or indirectly as a result of the use, application, or interpretation of the material in this book.

26366710R00020

Printed in Great Britain
by Amazon